I0390716

LAW ON ENVIRONMENTAL PROTECTION

Essential Legal Terms Explained You Need To Know About Law On Environmental Protection!

DR. PETER JOHNSON

ISBN: 9781093375824

TEXT COPYRIGHT © [DR. PETER JOHNSON]

2

Table of Contents

Introduction

Thank you and congratulate you for downloading the book *'LAW ON ENVIRONMENTAL PROTECTION: Essential Legal Terms Explained You Need To Know About Law On Environmental Protection!'*

With a clear, concise, and engaging writing style, Dr. Peter Johnson will help you with a practical understanding of food safety law topics about *principles of environmental protection, course of actions that are advised to take to protect the environment, prohibited acts, protection and sustainable development of forest resources, management of greenhouse gas emissions, management of ozone-depleting substances, renewable energy development, eco-friendly production and consumption, waste-to-energy process, management of land environmental quality, controlling of land environmental pollution, minimization and recycling of wastes, collecting and treating discarded products*; provide you a road map to navigating law on environmental protection rules and help you build a foundation for understanding the overall picture and **much much more**. This book delivers extensive coverage of every aspect of the law and details the duties a paralegal is expected to perform when working within law on environmental protection. High-level, comprehensive coverage is combined with cutting-edge developments and foundational concepts.

As the author of the book, I promise this book will be ***an invaluable source of legal reference for professionals, international lawyers, law students, business professionals*** and anyone else who want to improve their use of legal terminology, succinct clarification of legal terms and have a better understanding of law on lawyers. All legal terms and phrases are well written and explained clearly in plain English.

Thank you again for purchasing this book, and I hope you enjoy it.

Let's get started!

General Provisions

Law on environmental protection provides statutory provisions on environmental protection activities; measures and resources used for the purpose of environmental protection; rights, powers, duties and obligations of regulatory bodies, agencies, organizations, households and individuals who are tasked with the environmental protection task.

Interpretation Of Terms

1. *Environment* refers to a system of natural and artificial physical factors affecting the existence and development of human beings and creatures.

2. *Environment components* refer to physical constituent elements forming an integral part of the environment such as land, water, air, sound, light, organism and things in other physical forms.

3. *Environmental protection* refers to the environmental conservation, and the prevention and control of harmful impacts on environment; the response to environmental emergencies; the mitigation of environmental pollution, degradation, improvement and remediation; proper extraction and consumption of natural resources for the purpose of maintaining a pure environment.

4. *Sustainable development* refers to the formal process in which the development can help keep pace with rigorous needs that emerge at the present time without causing any harm to the likelihood of future generations' satisfying such needs on the basis of sustaining a close and harmonious cooperation amongst the economic growth, social progress and environmental protection.

5. *Technical regulations on environment* refer to a set of parameters relating to the environmental quality in surrounding areas, number of contaminants that remain in wastes, technical and managerial requirements which are issued by a competent regulatory authority in the form of a written document that entities involved must be binding on to serve the purpose of environmental protection.

6. *Environmental standards* refer to a set of parameters relating to the environmental quality in surrounding areas, number of contaminants that remain in wastes, technical and managerial requirements which are issued by a competent regulatory authority in the form of a written document that entities involved may choose to follow at their discretion to serve the purpose of environmental protection.

7. *Environmental health* refers to the state of physical factors in the environment that can affect the human health and cause human diseases.

8. *Environmental pollution* refers to the change in the environment components in breach of technical regulations on environment and environmental standards, which can result in adverse impacts on human beings and creatures.

9. *Environmental degradation* refers to a reduction in the quality and amount of environment components, which can pose a threat to human beings and creatures.

10. *Environmental emergencies* refer to any unexpected event that happens as a result of human activities or environmental changes, which can seriously contaminate, degrade or disturb the environment.

11. *Environmental contaminant* refers to chemicals, physical and biological substance, when introduced into the environment, that exceed the permitted benchmark, resulting in the environmental pollution.

12. *Wastes* refer to a kind of materials emitted from activities such as manufacturing, trading, service, daily activities and others.

13. *Hazardous wastes* refer to the waste that exhibits one or more of hazardous traits such as toxicity, reactivity, infectivity, ignitability, corrosivity or other poisonous characteristics.

14. *Environmental industry* refers to an economic sector that involves the supplying of technological solutions, equipment, services and products used to suit the requirements for environmental protection.

15. *Waste management* refers to the process of prevention, control, minimization, monitoring, classification, collection, transportation, reuse, recycling and disposition of wastes.

16. *Scrap* refers to materials that are collected, classified and selected from discarded materials and products during the manufacturing or consumption process, which can be then reused as materials for another manufacturing process.

17. *Environment's maximal load* refers to the maximum resistance of the environment against influential factors which can enable the environment itself to be remediated.

18. *Pollution control* refers to the process for preventing, detecting, controlling and removal of pollutants or contaminants.

19. *Environmental regulatory dossier* refers to a combination of documents on the environment and environmental protection processes and activities performed by agencies, organizations, and businesses in accordance with laws.

20. *Environmental monitoring* refers to the formal processes and activities that need to take place to monitor the quality and components of the environment in a systematic manner as well as factors affecting the environment in order to provide necessary information to prepare the assessment on current status and change of the environment quality, and harmful impacts on the environment.

21. *Planning for environmental protection* refers to the environmental zoning scheme to conserve, develop and establish technical infrastructural systems for the environmental protection in line with a range of measures to be taken to protect the environment, which must be closely connected with the general planning for socio-economic development to aim for the sustainable development.

22. *Strategic environmental assessment* refers to the analysis and forecast of existing or potential impacts on the environment, which have been described in the development strategy, planning and proposal, in order to provide measures to control and reduce adverse impacts on the environment, and to serve as a ground for and to be incorporated in such development strategy, planning and proposal with the objective of ensuring the sustainable development.

23. *Environmental impact assessment* refers to the analysis and prediction of environmental impacts of specific investment projects in order to take preventive measures to protect the environment during the implementation of such projects.

24. *Environmental protection infrastructure* refers to the system for collecting, storing, transporting, recycling, reusing and disposing waste substances and monitoring the environment.

25. *Greenhouse gas* refers to a gas in an atmosphere causing the global warming and climate change.

26. *Response to climate change* refers to actions that human beings may take to adapt to and mitigate the climate change.

27. *Carbon credit* refers to any tradable certificate or permit relating to a reduction in greenhouse gas emission.

28. *Environmental security* refers to the assurance about none of significant threats posed by environmental events and trends to the politic and social stability as well as the economic growth in a country.

29. *Environmental information* refers to environmental figures and data represented in the form of signs, letters, numbers, images, sounds or the like.

Principles Of Environmental Protection

1. Environmental protection is the responsibilities and obligations of every agency, organization, family household and individual.

2. Environmental protection must harmonize with the economic growth, social security, assurance about the children's right, promotion of gender equality, development and conservation of biodiversity, response to climate changes, in order to ensure the human right to live in a pure environment.

3. Environmental protection must be performed on the basis that natural resources are properly consumed and amount of waste substances are reduced to a minimum.

4. National environmental protection must conform to the regional and global environmental protection; environmental protection must ensure no harm to the national sovereignty and security.

5. Environmental protection must comply with the natural laws and characteristics, cultural and historical identities as well as the level of socio-economic development of the country.

6. Environmental protection activities must be carried out in a regular manner, and prioritize the prevention and control of environmental pollution, emergencies and degradation.

7. Any organization, family household or individual, who uses environment components and profits from the environment, is obliged to make their financial contribution to the environmental protection task.

8. Any organization, family household or individual, who causes environmental pollution, emergencies and degradation, is responsible to find remedial solutions, pay damages and assumes other responsibilities as stipulated by laws.

Regulatory Policies On The Environmental Protection

1. Facilitate the involvement of organizations, family households and individuals in the environmental protection activities; inspect and supervise the performance of environmental protection activities in accordance with laws.

2. Propagate, raise people's awareness of environmental protection in association with impose administrative punishments; introduce economic measure and others to reinforce statutes and etiquettes of the environmental protection.

3. Conserve the biological diversity; extract and use natural resources in a proper and economical manner; develop green and renewable energy; strengthen recycling, reuse and reduce waste substances to a minimum.

4. Prioritize the solutions to pressing environmental problems, serious environmental pollution and water contamination; enhance the environmental protection at residential areas and improve the environmental protection infrastructure.

5. Diversify investment funds for the environmental protection; reserve a specified amount of expenditures allocated from the government budget for the environmental protection, which equals to a gradual increase in the growth rate; perform the consistent management of funds for the environmental protection and prioritize the utilization of these funds for key industries in the environmental protection.

6. Provide financial and land preferences and supports for the environmental protection activities, environment-friendly manufacturers and businesses.

7. Intensify the training for workforce involved in the environmental protection task.

8. Increase the development of environmental technology and science; prioritize the study, transfer and application of technological advances, high and eco-friendly technologies; introduce environmental standards to better meet the requirements for the environmental protection.

9. Combine environmental and natural resource protection activities with the response to climate change and environmental security assurance.

10. Commend and reward agencies, organizations, family households and individuals for their active role in environmental protection activities.

11. Seek and enter into more international cooperation in the environmental protection; fulfill the international commitment to the environmental protection.

Course Of Actions That Are Advised To Take To Protect The Environment

1. Communicate, educate and mobilize people to participate in the environmental protection, keep the environment clean, protect natural landscapes and biodiversity.

2. Protect and use natural resources in an appropriate and cost-efficient manner.

3. Control, collect, reuse and recycle wastes.

4. Bring forth the response to climate change; develop and use green and renewable energy sources; make a reduction in the greenhouse gas emission and gases causing the ozone layer depletion.

5. File an application for registration as eco-friendly establishments and products; manufacture, trade and consume eco-friendly products.

6. Conduct scientific researches, technology transfer and apply the technology for the disposal and recycling of wastes, and environment-friendly technologies.

7. Invest in establishing plants for the production of devices and equipment used for the environmental protection; supply environmental protection services; carry out the environmental auditing; provide green credits and investments.

8. Conserve and develop indigenous genes; produce and import genetic resources which are of high economic value and environmental benefit.

9. Erect eco-friendly villages and hamlets at mountainous areas and minority communities, and residential zones.

10. Develop organizations and environmental sanitation services in various forms, which shall be autonomously managed by the residential community.

11. Form good life styles and habits towards the environmental sanitation; eradicate depraved customs that can pose risks to the environment.

12. Contribute intellectual, effort and financial contribution to environmental protection activities; enter into public-private partnership in the environmental protection.

Prohibited Acts

1. Ruin and illegally extract natural resources.

2. Obtain biotic resources by means of mass-killing equipment, devices and methods; carry out such production process in wrong seasons and in breach of legal regulations on the permitted productivity.

3. Obtain, trade and consume wild plants and animals identified in the list of preferentially-protected endangered, precious and scarce species, regulated by the competent authority.

4. Transport and bury poisons, radioactive substances, wastes and other hazardous substances in violation of technical process of the environmental protection.

5. Get rid of untreated wastes or sewage to meet the rigorous standards stipulated in technical regulations on environment; spread toxics, radioactive substances and other hazardous substances out to the land, water and air.

6. Discharge hazardous wastewater, waste substances and microorganisms and other poisonous agents which can impose risks to human beings and creatures into water sources.

7. Discharge smoke, dirt and gas containing toxic agents or smells into the air; emit the radiation, discharge the radioactivity and get substances to be exposed to the ionization, which exceeds the acceptable level stipulated in the technical regulations on environment.

8. Generate noises and vibrations in excess of the acceptable level stipulated in the technical regulations on environment.

9. Import and transit waste substances from overseas countries in any form.

10. Import and transit untested animals, plants, and microorganisms that are not identified in the list of permitted species.

11. Manufacture and trade products likely to pose risks to human beings, creatures and ecology; manufacture and utilize raw materials and building materials containing toxic agents in excess of the acceptable level prescribed in the technical regulations on environment.

12. Sabotage or infringe upon natural heritage sites and wildlife sanctuaries.

13. Wreck structures, equipment and facilities used for environmental protection activities.

14. Carry out illegal operations and live in areas defined as banned areas by the competent authority due to their seriously dangerous environment for human beings.

15. Conceal acts of environmental depletion as well as interfere with the environmental protection and misrepresent the information that can cause bad effects on the environment.

16. Abuse the power or authority, or overuse powers or lack responsibilities of the competent entities to infringe upon the regulations on environmental management.

Principle, Level And Term Of The Planning For Environmental Protection

Planning for environmental protection must comply with the following principles:

a) Conform to the natural, socio-economic conditions; the general strategy and planning for the socio-economic development, and national defense and security maintenance; the national environment protection strategy with the aim of ensuring the sustainable development;

b) Ensure the conformity to the planning for land use; keep basic contents given in the planning for environmental protection consistent;

c) Ensure the conformity to principles of environmental protection.

Objects That Require The Formulation Of Environmental Protection Plan

1. Investment projects that are not identified as objects that require the environmental impact assessment.

2. Alternatives for the production, trading and services that are not identified as objects that require the formulation of investment projects in accordance with the law on investment.

3. Details of this Article shall be regulated by the Government.

Environmental Protection Concerns During The Inspection, Assessment And Preparation Of The Planning For Utilization Of Natural Resources And Biodiversity

1. The current status, recyclability and economic value of natural resources and biodiversity must be investigated and evaluated to serve as a basis for the preparation of the plan for proper utilization; define the limit on permitted extraction levels, severance tax rates, environmental protection fees, environmental remediation deposits, biodiversity reimbursable costs, environmental damages and other measures for the environmental protection.

2. The inspection, assessment and preparation of the planning for utilization of natural resources must be performed in accordance with laws.

Protection And Sustainable Development Of Forest Resources

All activities relating to production, trading and service provision as well as others that cause impacts on land, water, air resources and forest-related biodiversity must comply with regulations set out in Law on environmental protection and the law on biodiversity, protection and development of forests, and other relevant laws.

Environmental Protection Concerns During The Basic Survey, Exploration, Extraction And Utilization Of Natural Resources

1. The basic survey, exploration, extraction and utilization of natural resources must comply with the planning approved by competent regulatory agencies.

2. A permit for exploration, extraction and utilization of natural resources must enclose the information about environmental protection in accordance with laws.

3. In course of basic survey, exploration, extraction and utilization of natural resources, interested organizations and individuals bear responsibility for fulfilling the requirements for environmental protection; must carry out the environmental remediation in accordance with Law on environmental protection and other relevant laws.

Environmental Protection Concerns During The Exploration, Extraction And Processing Of Minerals

1. In course of prospecting, extraction and processing of minerals, interested organizations or individuals must find preventive measures and responses to environmental emergencies and meet requirements for environmental protection, rehabilitation and remediation as follows:

a) Collect and dispose of wastewater in accordance with laws;

b) Collect and dispose of solid wastes in accordance with the regulations on solid waste management;

c) Take measures to prevent and control the spread of hazardous waste dusts and emissions that can pose threats to the surroundings;

d) Draw up a plan for environmental rehabilitation and remediation for all processes of exploration, extraction and processing of minerals, and take ongoing action to rehabilitate and restore the environment in course of exploration, extraction and processing of minerals;

dd) Provide environmental remediation deposits in accordance with laws.

2. Minerals with hazardous properties must be handled and shipped by dedicated transports and properly covered to prevent being spread out to the environment.

3. Employment of machinery and equipment that can cause harmful impacts on the environment, hazardous chemicals in the mineral exploration and extraction is subject to the examination and inspection carried out by the agency in charge of State management of environmental protection.

4. Prospecting, extraction, shipping and processing of petroleum and minerals that contain radioactive, toxic and explosive agents must conform to regulations set out in Law on environmental protection and the law on chemical safety, radiation safety and nuclear safety.

General Provisions On The Response To Climate Change

1. All activities relating to the environmental protection must be harmoniously connected with the response to climate change.

2. Organizations or individuals shall be responsible to fulfill requirements for the environmental protection and response to climate change during their production, trading and service provision as stipulated in Law on environmental protection and other relevant laws.

3. Ministries, and quasi-ministerial organs shall design and develop the action plan for the environmental protection and response to climate change within their area of competence.

Integration Of Main Contents Of Responses To Climate Change With The Strategy, Planning And Proposal For Socio-Economic Development

1. Main contents of response to climate change must be included in the strategy, planning, proposal for socio-economic development as well as planning for industrial and sectoral development, which is applicable to objects required to make a report on strategic environment assessment as prescribed in Law on environmental protection.

2. The integration of main contents of responses to climate change into the strategy, planning and proposal for socio-economic development as well as planning for industrial and sectoral development must rely on the assessment of correlation of activities described in the strategy, planning and proposal with the environment, climate change, and a range of measures to be taken for the environmental protection and response to climate change.

Management Of Greenhouse Gas Emissions

Management of greenhouse gas emissions shall be described as follows:

a) Setting the national regulations on the inventorying of greenhouse gases;

b) Taking action to reduce the harmful impact of greenhouse gases in conformity with socio-economic conditions;

c) Managing the forest resources in a sustainable manner, conserving and increasing forest carbon stock, protecting and fostering ecosystems;

d) Examining and inspecting the compliance with regulations on inventorying and reducing greenhouse gas emissions;

dd) Creating and developing carbon credit markets in the country, and participating in carbon credit markets in the globe;

e) Entering into the international cooperation in an effort to reduce greenhouse gases.

Management Of Ozone-Depleting Substances

1. Prioritize the introduction and implementation of policies on and plans for management, mitigation and elimination of ozone-depleting substances.

2. Prohibit the production, importation, temporary importation and re-exportation as well as consumption of ozone-depleting substances.

Renewable Energy Development

1. Renewable energy refers to energy that comes from resources such as water, wind, sunlight, geothermal heat, tides, waves, biological fuels and other resources that can generate renewable energy.

2. Promote the production, importation and employment of renewable energy-driven machinery, equipment and means of transport.

Eco-Friendly Production And Consumption

1. Agencies, organizations, family households or individuals shall be responsible to manufacture and consume eco-friendly products and services.

2. The Head of state budget-funded institutions shall bear their responsibility for preferring eco-friendly products and services that have been recognized as ecolabels under legal regulations.

Waste-To-Energy Process

1. Owner of manufacturing or business establishments must be responsible for reducing, reusing and recycling wastes, and generating the energy from wastes.

2. The Government shall provide preferential policies on the mitigation, reuse and recycling of wastes, and generation of the energy from wastes.

Rights And Responsibilities Of The Human Community For The Response To Climate Change

1. Human community shall be vested with the right to provide and request the provision of information about climate change issues, exclusive of information specified in the list of state secret information.

2. Human community shall be responsible for participating in activities relating to the response to climate change.

3. The regulatory agency in charge of climate change issues shall bear responsibility for providing information and create events to raise people's awareness of climate change as well as provide better supports to human communities to get involved in activities relating to the response to climate change.

Development And Application Of Technological And Scientific Advances For The Response To Climate Change

1. All activities relating to the study, transfer and application of technological and scientific advances for the response to climate change shall be given priority, including:

a) Developing a single scientific discipline or a combination of scientific disciplines of the management, assessment, supervision and prediction of impacts caused by climate change on the socio-economic growth, environmental issues and community health;

b) Conduct basic and applied scientific investigation and research; develop and transfer technological advances in reducing greenhouse gases and coping with climate change; enhance the competitiveness of the economy, key manufacturing industries; promote the development of low carbon economy and green growth.

2. Agencies, organizations and manufacturing or business establishment shall be responsible for conducting or engaging in scientific and technological researches, transfer and application with the aim of responding to the climate change.

International Cooperation In The Response To Climate Change

The State shall introduce policies on international cooperation in attracting more investments, financial aids, develop and transfer technologies, and enhance its competence in taking measures to respond to the climate change with the aim of building a green economy in the future.

General Provisions On The Protection Of Marine And Island Environment

1. Strategy, planning and proposal for the socio-economic development, national defense and security relating to sea and islands must include environmental protection and response to climate change.

2. Waste sources discharged from mainland, islands and marine activities must be controlled, prevented, mitigated and disposed in accordance with laws.

3. Prevention and response to environmental emergencies that take place on the sea and islands require the close cooperation between regulatory bodies, rescue teams and other relevant entities.

4. Organizations or individuals operating on the sea and islands must take the initiative in responding to environmental emergencies and bear their responsibility for working with regulatory bodies and other interested entities to respond to environmental emergencies that occur on the sea and islands.

5. Strategy, planning and proposal for the extraction of natural resources from marine zones, islands, wildlife sanctuaries, mangrove forest, natural and island heritage sites must align with the strategy and planning for environmental protection.

Controlling And Processing Of Marine And Island Environment Pollution

1. Waste substances discharged from the mainland to the seas and derived from the sea and islands must be statistically reported, assessed and subject to any measure to be taken to prevent, reduce and dispose them to achieve accepted standards set out in the technical regulations on environment.

2. Oil, fat, drilling fluids, ballast water, chemicals and other hazardous substances after being used for activities on the sea and islands must be collected, stored, transported and disposed in accordance with regulations on waste management.

3. Dumping and discharge of wastes on the marine zones and islands must be based on the specific features and attributes of wastes and must be permitted by the competent regulatory agencies.

Prevention Of And Response To Marine And Island Environmental Emergencies

1. Organizations or individuals whose activities on the sea and islands can pose a threat to causing environmental emergencies must set up plan and prepare resources to prevent and respond to environmental emergencies as well as send a report to regulatory agencies.

2. Ministries, quasi-ministerial agencies, and Governmental organs within their powers and jurisdiction must be responsible for promptly alerting and notifying any marine environmental emergency as well as take responsive and remedial measures.

General Provisions On The Environmental Protection For River Water

1. The environmental protection for river water is one of basic requirements set out in the planning and proposal for extraction and utilization of river water.

2. Waste discharges drained out to the river basin must be managed to meet the accepted standards of river's maximal load.

3. The quality of river water and sediments must be monitored and assessed.

4. The environmental protection for the river basin must be closely connected with the biodiversity conservation, river water extraction and utilization.

5. Owners of manufacturing or business establishments, family households and individuals must be responsible for reducing and disposing of waste substances before being discharged to the river basin as stipulated by laws.

Processes For Monitoring And Controlling The River-Water Environmental Pollution

1. Make a statistical report, assess, mitigate and dispose of wastes discharged to the river basin.

2. Carry out the periodical monitoring and assessment of the quality of river water and sediments.

3. Investigate and assess the river's maximal load; publicize river sections or rivers that are no longer capable of loading waste substances; determine the limited amount of wastes discharged to the river.

4. Control pollution conditions and improve the environmental condition for contaminated river sections or rivers.

5. Conduct the trans-border monitoring and assessment of the environmental quality of river water and sediments, and share necessary information on the basis of complying with international laws and practices.

6. Develop and become involved in the initiative for the river environmental protection.

7. Disclose the information about river water and sediment environment to the organization specializing in the management, extraction and utilization of river water.

Responsibility Of Provincial People's Committees For The Environmental Protection For Water Derived From Provincial Rivers

1. Disclose the information about waste discharges into rivers.

2. Direct and arrange activities to prevent and control waste discharges drained to the river.

3. Conduct the assessment of the river's maximal load; determine the limited amount of wastes discharged to the river; publicize river sections or rivers that are no longer capable of loading waste substances.

4. Carry out the assessment of loss incurred by the river-water environmental pollution and the control of such pollution conditions.

5. Direct the formulation and development of the initiative for the river environmental protection.

Responsibility Of The Ministry Of Natural Resources And Environment For The River-Water Environmental Protection

1. Assess the quality of river water and sediments at inter-provincial and trans-border rivers.

2. Investigate and assess the river's maximal load, determine the limited amount of waste discharges which corresponds to the objective of using water and making the related information known to the public.

3. Issue and provide guidance for the implementation of technical regulations on river-water and sediment environment.

4. Issue and provide guidance for the assessment of the river's maximal load and quota of sewage discharged to the inter-provincial rivers, control the pollution condition and improve the environmental health for contaminated river and river sections.

5. Arrange and direct activities that should be performed for the purpose of the environmental protection for inter-provincial river water.

6. Conduct the assessment of the polluting waste discharges, damaging levels and take measures to control the pollution condition for inter-provincial rivers.

7. Make a final report on the information about the quality of river water and sediments and send an annual report on this matter to the Prime Minister.

8. Prepare and submit the initiative for the water environmental protection for inter-provincial rivers to the Prime Minister to seek an approval.

Environmental Protection For Lake, Pond, Canal And Ditch Water

1. The reserve and quality of lake, pond, canal and ditch water sources must be investigated, assessed and protected for the purpose of water moderation.

2. Lake, pond, canal and ditch located in the urban and residential area must be renovated and protected to meet the requirements set out in the planning.

3. Organizations or individuals do not allow to encroach upon and illegally erect houses and structures on the water surface or near lake, pond, canal and ditch; restrict the sand-filling of lake and pond in the urban and residential area.

4. Provincial People's Committees take responsibility for investigating and assessing the reserve and quality of water as well as set up plans for protection and moderation of water flows on lake, pond, canal and ditch; formulate and develop the plan for renovation or relocation of residential zones, clusters and structures built on the lake, pond, canal and ditch that can cause environmental pollution and block the water current as well as degrade the wetland environment and ruin urban landscapes.

Environmental Protection For Water Reservoirs Or Lakes For The Purpose Of Irrigation And Hydropower

1. The construction, management and operation of water reservoirs or lakes for the purpose of irrigation and hydropower must meet the requirement for the environmental protection.

2. Do not encroach upon the land area and dump solid wastes, lands and stones out to lakes; drain wastewater that has not been treated properly as required by the technical regulations on environment into the lake.

3. The agency in charge of water reservoirs or lakes for the purpose of irrigation and hydropower shall be responsible to conduct the tri-monthly environmental monitoring for lake water.

Environmental Protection For Underground Water

1. Only allow to use permitted chemical in the approved list released by the competent regulatory agency in course of prospecting and extraction of underground water.

2. Take preventive measures against the pollution of underground water through prospecting and extraction wells. Underground water facilities must be responsible for environmental remediation at prospecting and extraction sites. Abandoned exploration and extraction drill holes must be refilled in compliance with proper technical process.

3. Production, trading and service provision facilities that employ harmful chemicals and radioactive substances must apply preventive measures against leakage and spread out to the underground water.

4. Chemical sheds, treatment facilities and landfills of hazardous wastes must be developed to ensure technical safety, and apply necessary measures to barricade harmful chemicals absorbed into the underground water in accordance with legal regulations.

5. Organizations or individuals who contaminate the underground water must assume their responsibility for dealing with the underground water pollution.

General Provisions On The Environmental Protection For Land

1. The environmental protection is one of fundamental requirements for the management of land resource.

2. Sketch out the planning, proposal, project and action plan for the land utilization must consider the impact on land environment and introduce measures to protect the land environment.

3. Organization, family household and individual who is vested with the land ownership is obliged to perform the land environmental protection.

4. Organization, family household and individual who pollutes the land environment shall be liable to carry out the treatment, renovation and remediation of land environment.

Management Of Land Environmental Quality

1. Land environmental quality must be investigated, assessed, classified and managed as well as disclose relevant information to organizations and individuals involved.

2. Wastes discharged into the land environment are not allowed to exceed the land's maximal load.

3. Land areas faced with the degradation must be confined to being expanded, tracked and monitored.

4. Degraded land areas must be rehabilitated and restored.

5. The regulatory agency in charge of the environmental protection must be responsible for investigating, assessing and disclosing relevant information about the land environmental quality.

Controlling Of Land Environmental Pollution

1. Elements that can pose a risk of polluting the land environment must be defined, statistically reported, assessed and controlled.

2. The regulatory agencies in charge of the environmental protection shall be responsible for taking necessary measures to control the land pollution.

3. Manufacturing or business establishments shall be responsible for applying measures to control the environmental pollution thereat.

4. Land areas containing soil and mud exposed to the dioxin agent which is derived from the herbicide used in the war time, remains of plant pesticides and other hazardous substances must be investigated, assessed, restricted and disposed in order to meet the required standards set out in the environmental protection regulations.

General Provisions On The Aerial Environment Protection

1. All waste gases discharged into the aerial environment must be assessed and controlled.

2. Organizations or individuals involving in the harmful gas emission that causes bad effects on the environment during their production, trading and service provision activities must be responsible for reducing and disposing of such waste gases in order to meet the accepted standards for aerial environment as stipulated by laws.

Management Of Aerial Environment Quality

The regulatory agency in charge of the environmental protection shall take their responsibility for monitoring and assessing the quality of aerial environment as well as disclose relevant information hereof; where the air pollution is detected, a prompt alert and solution must be in place.

Controlling Of Aerial Environment Pollution

1. Waste gas emission source must be determined in respect of amount, properties and features of these emissions.

2. The examination and approval of projects and operations that emit waste gases must depend on the aerial environment's maximal load and ensure none of threats to human and environmental health.

3. Manufacturing or business establishments that are likely to emit a large amount of industrial waste gases must register polluting sources, measure, statistically report, inventory and set up database relating to the amount, characteristics and properties of waste emissions.

4. Manufacturing or business establishments that are own the large source of industrial emissions must install the automatic and non-stop waste-gas monitoring equipment and must be licensed by the relevant competent authority.

Environmental Protection In Economic Zones

1. Every economic zone must have infrastructure works serving environmental protection as prescribed by law.

2. Every management board of economic zones must have a unit specialized in environmental protection.

3. The management boards of economic zones shall cooperate with local regulatory bodies in organizing environmental protection and shall report the environmental protection tasks in economic zones as prescribed by law.

Environmental Protection In Industrial Parks, Export-Processing Zones, And Hi-Tech Zones

1. Management boards of industrial parks, export-processing zones, and hi-tech zones shall cooperate with local regulatory bodies in inspecting environmental protection tasks and report the environmental protection tasks in their industrial parks, export-processing zones, and hi-tech zones as prescribed by law.

2. Management boards of industrial parks, export-processing zones, and hi-tech zones must have units specialized in environmental protection.

3. Investors in industrial parks, export-processing zones, and hi-tech zones must satisfy the requirements below:

a) The zoning and operations must be suitable for environmental protection tasks;

b) The concentrated wastewater collection and treatment system are conformable with environmental regulations; there is an automatic and continuous wastewater monitoring system as well as wastewater flow rate meters.

c) Appropriate units are assigned to take charge of environmental protection tasks.

Environmental Protection In Industrial Complexes And Concentrated Business Zones

1. Investors in industrial complexes and concentrated business zones must perform the following environmental protection tasks:

a) Formulate an environmental protection plan;

b) Invest in a wastewater collection and treatment system that meet environmental standards;

c) Carry out environmental monitoring as prescribed by law;

d) Assign employees in charge of environmental protection.

2. Management boards of concentrated business zones shall perform the environmental protection tasks below:

a) Formulate an environmental protection plan;

b) Invest in a wastewater and solid waste collection and treatment system that meet environmental standards;

c) Assign employees in charge of environmental protection.

3. The People's Committees of districts are obliged to:

a) Inspect the formulation and implementation of environmental protection plans in industrial complexes and concentrated business zones;

b) Submit reports on environmental protection in industrial complexes and concentrated business zones to competent authorities.

Environmental Protection In Manufacturing And Business Establishments

1. Manufacturing and business establishments are obliged to:

a) Collect and treat wastewater in accordance with environmental standards;

b) Collect, classify, store, treat, and discharge solid waste in accordance with law;

c) Minimize, collect, treat dust and exhaust gases in accordance with law; ensure no leakage and discharge of noxious gases into the environment; limit noise, vibration, light and heat emission that negatively affects the surrounding environment and employees;

d) Provide sufficient resources and equipment for prevention and response to environmental emergencies;

dd) Formulate and implement environmental protection plans;

2. Manufacturing establishments or warehouses must ensure that there are no negative impacts on residential areas if they:

a) Have inflammable and/or explosive substances;

b) Have radioactive substances or strongly radiating substances;

c) Have substances that are harmful to humans and animals;

d) Emit dust, smell, noise that negatively affect human health;

dd) Cause pollution to water sources.

3. Manufacturing and business establishments that produce a large amount of waste that is likely to seriously affect the environment must specialized units or employees specialized in environmental protection; the environment management systems of which must be certified as prescribed by the government.

Environmental Protection In Agricultural Production

1. Every entity that produces, imports, sells, and/or uses pesticides and veterinary medicines must comply with environmental protection regulations.

2. Expired fertilizers, products for breeding environment remediation; containers of fertilizers, pesticides and veterinary medicine must be treated after use in accordance with waste management regulations.

3. Every concentrated breeding zone must have an environmental protection plan and:

a) Ensure environmental hygienic of the residential areas;

b) Collect, treat wastewater and solid wastes in accordance with waste management regulations;

c) Periodically clean the farms, pens to prevent, and response to epidemics;

d) Deal with dead animals in accordance with regulations on hazardous waste management and preventive medicine.

Environmental Protection In Trade Villages

1. Every trade villages are obliged to:

a) Have an environmental protection plan;

b) Have infrastructure works for collecting, classifying, storing, treating, and discharging wastes in accordance with environmental standards;

c) Has an autonomous unit in charge of environmental protection.

2. Manufacturing establishments involved in the trades encouraged by the government in trade villages are obliged to:

a) Formulate and implement environmental protection plans as prescribed by law;

b) Take measures to minimize noise, vibration, light, dust, heat, exhaust gases, wastewater; tackle pollution on the spot; collect, classify, store, and treat solid wastes as prescribed by law.

Environmental Protection In Aquaculture

1. Every entity that produces, imports, and/or sells aquacultural medicines or chemicals must comply with environmental protection regulations and relevant regulations of law.

2. Do not use aquacultural medicines or chemicals that are expired or not on the list of permissible substances in aquaculture.

3. Expired aquaculture medicines and chemicals; used containers of aquaculture medicines and chemicals, mud and feed that deposit while cleaning must be collected and treated in accordance with waste management regulations.

4. Concentrated aquaculture zones must be conformable with planning and satisfy the following requirements:

b) Wastes are collected and treated in accordance with law;

b) The environment is remedied after aquaculture is terminated;

c) Environmental hygiene condition and prevention of aquacultural epidemics are ensured; no harmful chemicals or deposits are used.

5. The concentrated aquaculture zone is not built on an alluvial ground that is forming an estuary.

6. Mangrove forests are not destroyed to serve aquaculture.

Environmental Protection In Hospitals And Medical Facilities

1. Hospitals and medical facilities are obliged to:

a) Collect and treat medical wastewater in accordance with environmental standards;

b) Classify solid biomedical waste at source; collect, transport, store, and treat medical solid waste in accordance with environmental standards;

c) There are plans and equipment for prevention and response to environmental emergencies;

d) Biomedical wastes must be preliminarily treated to eliminate pathogens that are likely to spread before wastes are stored, treated, or destroyed at a gathering site.

dd) Exhaust gases are treated in accordance with environmental standards;

2. Radiation facilities and medical equipment using radioactive substances must comply with regulations of law on radiation safety and nuclear safety.

3. Investors in hospitals and medical facilities shall provide sufficient funding to build sanitary works, waste collection, storage, and treatment systems that satisfy environmental protection requirements.

Environmental Protection In Construction

1. Construction planning must comply with regulations on environmental protection.

2. Waste treatment works must be included in the construction design and budget of the construction of manufacturing and business establishments that produce wastes negatively impact the environment.

3. Construction must satisfy the following environmental protection requirements:

a) Measures are taken to ensure that the construction sites in residential areas do not produce dust, heat, noise, vibration, and light beyond environmental standards;

b) Building materials are transported with suitable vehicles that ensure no leakage or environmental pollution;

c) Solid wastes and other wastes are collected and treated in accordance with environmental standards.

Environmental Protection In Transport

1. Traffic planning must comply with regulations on environmental protection.

2. Motor vehicles must be certified as conformable with environmental standards by registry authorities before they are put into operation.

3. Vehicles used for transporting raw materials and wastes must be covered while they are using public roads in order to avoid leakage and pollution.

4. Organizations and individuals involved in transport of dangerous goods must have qualifications in environmental protection as prescribed by law.

5. The transport of goods at risk of environmental emergencies must satisfy the following requirements:

a) Specialized equipment and vehicles are used to ensure no leakage or discharge;

b) A license to transport is issued by a competent authority;

c) The route and time are conformable with the license.

Environmental Protection In Goods Import And Transit

1. Machinery, equipment, vehicles, raw materials, fuel, chemicals, and goods imported or in transit must satisfy environmental protection requirements.

2. The following machinery, equipment, vehicles, raw materials, fuel, chemicals, and goods are banned from import:

a) Machinery, equipment, and vehicles that fail to comply with environmental protection requirements;

b) Machinery, equipment, and vehicles that are used and intended to be disassembled;

c) Raw materials, fuel, chemicals, and goods on the list of goods banned from import;

d) Machinery, equipment, and vehicles contaminated with radioactive substances, bacteria, and other poisonous substances that have not been cleaned or cannot be cleaned;

dd) Food, food ingredients, food additives, food containers that are expired or not conformable with food safety regulations;

e) Medicines, ingredients of medicines used for human, veterinary medicines, pesticides that are expired or not conformable with food safety regulations.

3. The import of used ships must comply with environmental standards. The Government shall specify the permissible importers and conditions for importing, disassembling used ships.

Environmental Protection During Festivals And In The Tourism Industry

1. Every entity that manages or operates tourist attractions, resorts, and lodging establishments must:

a) Post the regulations on environmental protection at the tourist attractions and provide instructions;

b) Adequately and rationally install sanitary facilities and waste collection systems;

c) Appoint employees in charge of environmental hygiene.

2. Visitors to tourist attractions, lodging establishments, and festivals must:

a) Comply with the regulations on environmental protection at the tourist attractions or lodging establishments;

b) Discard wastes properly;

c) Keep public hygiene;

d) Not to infringe upon the landscape, relics and animals at the tourist attractions or lodging establishments.

Environmental Protection With Regard To Chemicals, Pesticides, And Veterinary Medicines

1. Every entity that produces, imports, sells, uses, transports, stores, transfers, and/or processes chemicals, pesticides, and/or veterinary medicines must comply with environmental protection regulations and relevant regulations of law.

2. Chemicals, pesticides, and veterinary medicines with high toxicity, stability, likely to spread or agglomerate in the environment and negatively impact the environment and human health must be registered, managed, assessed, and processed in accordance with law.

Environmental Protection By Research Institutes And Laboratories

1. Research institutes and laboratories must:

a) Collect and treat medical wastewater in accordance with environmental standards;

b) Classify solid wastes at sources; collect and treat solid wastes in accordance with regulations of law on solid waste management;

c) Process, destroy test specimens and chemicals in accordance with environmental standards;

d) Make plans and provide equipment for prevention and response to environmental emergencies.

2. Every research institute and laboratory that uses radioactive substances must comply with regulations of law on radiation safety and nuclear safety.

Environmental Protection Requirements Applied To Urban Areas And Residential Areas

1. Urban environmental protection must ensure sustainable development associated with sustention of natural, cultural, historical elements and the proportion of green space according to planning.

2. The infrastructural works serving environmental protection are uniform and conformable with the urban planning approved by a competent authority.

3. There are adequate equipment, vehicles and places for classifying wastes at source, collecting, gathering domestic solid wastes, and receiving wastes classified by households therein.

4. Ensure urban landscape, environmental hygiene; public sanitation works are installed.

5. Investors in concentrated residential area projects and apartment buildings shall fulfill the environmental protection requirements.

6. Scattered residential areas must have places and system for collecting and treating wastes, clean water supply systems, and activities to develop a green, clean, and safe environment.

Environmental Protection In Public Places

1. Organizations, households, and individuals are responsible for complying with environmental protection regulations and keep public hygiene; classify wastes and put them into public trashcans or permissible dumpsites; do not let domestic animals spoil public hygiene.

2. Managers of parks, amusement parks, tourist resorts, markets, train stations, bus stations, ports, ferry terminals, and other public places shall:

a) Appoint employees to collect wastes and clean the environment under their management;

b) Provide public sanitation works; equipment and vehicles for collecting wastes to ensure environmental hygiene;

c) Post public hygiene regulations.

Environmental Protection Requirements Applied To Households

1. Minimize, classify wastes at source; collect and take wastes to proper places.

2. Minimize, process, and discharge domestic sewages at proper places.

3. Do not emit exhaust gases, make noises, vibration, and other impacts beyond the limits in environmental standards, which cause negative impacts to the local community.

4. Pay environmental protection fees sufficiently and punctually; pay fees for wastes collection and waste treatment services as prescribed by law;

5. Participate in public environmental protection tasks.

6. The sanitation works and breeding farms must ensure hygiene and safety.

Autonomous Environmental Protection Organizations

1. Communities are encouraged by the State to establish local autonomous environmental protection organizations.

2. Autonomous environmental protection organizations are established and operated voluntarily in accordance with law to perform the following tasks:

a) Urge households and individuals to comply with regulations on hygiene and environmental protection;

b) Organize the collection, gathering, and treatment of wastes;

c) Keep environmental hygiene in the residential area and public places;

d) Formulate and organize the implementation of environmental protection commitments; encourage the people to give up unsound customs and bad habits that are harmful for health and the environment;

d) Participate in supervision of adherence to regulations of law on environmental protection of local manufacturing and business establishments.

Environmental Protection During Burial And Cremation

1. Every burial and cremation site must:

a) Comply with the planning;

b) Its location and distance satisfy the requirements with regard to environmental hygiene and landscape of the residential area;

c) Not pollute water sources and the surroundings.

2. Dead bodies and remains shall be treated, transported, and buried in accordance with environmental hygiene requirements.

3. The burial of people who die of dangerous epidemics shall comply with regulations of the Ministry of Health.

4. Provider of burial services must comply with regulations of law on environmental protection and infection control.

5. The State recommends that cremation and burial be carried out in cemeteries according to planning and unsound customs that cause environmental pollution be given up.

Requirements Applied To Waste Management

1. Wastes must be managed throughout the process of generation, minimization, classification, collection, transport, recycling, and destruction.

2. Conventional wastes that contain hazardous wastes beyond permissible limits and cannot be classified shall be managed in accordance with hazardous waste.

3. The Government shall elaborate regulations on waste management.

Minimization And Recycling Of Wastes

1. Wastes that can be recycled and used as energy must be classified.

2. Owners of manufacturing and business organizations that produce wastes are responsible for minimizing, recycling wastes, or transfer wastes to the organizations capable of recycling such wastes.

Collecting And Treating Discarded Products

1. Owners manufacturing and business establishments must collect and treat discarded products.

2. Users are responsible for taking discarded products to proper places.

3. The People's Committees and environment authorities shall facilitate manufacturing and business establishments to collect discarded products.

Responsibilities Of The People's Committees For Waste Management

The People's Committees, within the area of their competence, are obliged to:

1. Formulate, approve and implement planning for local waste treatment infrastructure.
2. Invest in and operate public works serving local waste management.
3. Introduce incentive policies to support waste management as prescribed by law.

Responsibilities Of Investors In Industrial Parks, Export-Processing Zones, Hi-Tech Zones For Waste Management

1. Provide sufficient areas for gathering wastes under their management.

2. Develop and operate concentrated sewage treatment systems.

Document Compilation, Registration And Licensing Of Hazardous Waste Treatment

1. Every entity that discharges hazardous wastes shall compile documents about hazardous wastes and apply for registration with an environment authority.

2. Only capable and licensed entities may process hazardous wastes.

Classification, Collection, And Storage Of Hazardous Wastes Prior To Processing

1. Every entity that discharges hazardous wastes must collect, store, and process hazardous wastes in accordance with environmental standards; if the entity that discharges hazardous wastes fails to process hazardous wastes in accordance with environmental standards, hazardous wastes shall be transferred to an entity licensed to process hazardous wastes.

2. Hazardous wastes must be kept in specialized containers that ensure no negative impacts on humans and the environment.

Transport Of Hazardous Wastes

1. Hazardous wastes must be transported with suitable vehicles and equipment which are specified in the license to process hazardous wastes.

2. Hazardous wastes transported to another country must comply with the international agreements.

Conditions Of Facilities That Process Hazardous Wastes

1. Its location is approved by a competent authority.

2. Its distance ensures no negative impacts on the environment and human.

3. There are technologies and specialized equipment for storing and processing hazardous waste in accordance with environmental standards.

4. There are constructions and measures for environmental protection.

5. There are managers granted certificates and qualified technicians.

6. There are procedures for safe operation of specialized equipment.

7. There is an environmental protection plan.

8. There is a plan for environmental remediation after shutdown.

Waste Management Contents In Environmental Protection Planning

1. Assessment and forecast for sources and amount of hazardous wastes.

2. Ability to collect and classify at source.

3. Ability to recycle.

4. Locations and scale of the gathering, recycling, and processing sites.

5. Hazardous waste processing technologies.

6. Resources

7. Schedule.

8. Task assignment.

Responsibility To Classify Conventional Solid Wastes

Owners of manufacturing and business establishments, organizations, households, and individuals that produce conventional solid wastes are responsible for classifying them at source to facilitate their recycling and processing.

Collection And Transport Of Conventional Solid Wastes

1. Conventional solid wastes shall be collected, stored, and transported with specialized vehicles and equipment.

2. Environment authorities shall organize the collection, storage, and transport of conventional solid wastes locally.

Recycling And Treating Conventional Solid Wastes

Owners of manufacturing and business establishments, organizations, households, and individuals that produce conventional solid wastes are responsible for recycling and treating them. If conventional solid wastes cannot be recycled or treated, they shall be sent to the organizations capable of recycling such or processing such wastes.

Conventional Solid Waste Management Contents In Environmental Protection Planning

1. Assessment and forecast for sources and amount of conventional solid wastes.

2. Ability to collect and classify at source.

3. Ability to recycle.

4. Location and scale of the gathering, recycling, and processing sites.

5. Conventional solid waste treatment technologies

6. Resources

7. Schedule.

8. Task assignment.

General Regulations On Wastewater Management

1. Wastewater shall be collected and treated in accordance with environmental standards.

2. Wastewater that contains hazardous elements beyond the permissible limits shall be managed in accordance with regulations on hazardous wastes

Collection And Treatment Of Wastewater

1. Every urban area and concentrated residential area must have a system for separating rainwater and wastewater.

2. Wastewater produced by manufacturing and business establishments must be collected and treated in accordance with environmental standards.

3. Waste sludge from wastewater treatment systems shall be managed in accordance with regulations of law on solid waste management; waste sludge that contains hazardous wastes beyond permissible limits and shall be managed in accordance with hazardous wastes.

Sewage Treatment System

1. The following entities must have sewage treatment systems:

a) Concentrated manufacturing/business zones;

b) Trade villages complexes;

c) Manufacturing and business establishments that are not connected to any concentrated sewage treatment systems.

2. Every sewage treatment system must:

a) Have a technology process suitable for the type of wastewater that needs treating;

b) Have a treatment capacity that is sufficient for the amount of wastewater produced;

c) Treat wastewater according to environmental standards;

d) Has the wastewater discharge outlets located at positions convenient for inspection and supervision;

dd) Be operated regularly.

3. The manager of the sewage treatment system shall carry out periodic monitory before and after the treatment. Monitory data shall be kept as the basis for sewage treatment system inspection.

4. Manufacturing and business establishments that produce a large amount of wastewater that is likely to harm the environment must carry out automatic environmental monitoring send data to competent authorities as prescribed by the Ministry of Natural Resources and Environment.

Management And Control Of Dust And Exhaust Gases

1. Any entity that produces dust and/or exhaust gases during their business operation shall take measures to control and treat dust/exhaust gases in accordance with environmental standards.

2. Vehicles, machinery, equipment, constructions that produce dust and/or exhaust gases must have filters, covers, or other parts to minimize exhaust gases and reduce dust in accordance with environmental standards.

3. Dust and exhaust gases that contain hazardous elements beyond the permissible limits shall be managed in accordance with regulations on hazardous wastes.

Management And Control Of Noise, Vibration, Light, And Radiation

1. Any entity that creates noise, vibration, light, and/or radiation must take measures to control and treat them in accordance with environmental standards.

2. Manufacturing and business establishments in residential areas that create noise must take measures to minimize them to avoid affecting the local community.

3. Managers of the routes with heavy traffic that produces noise, vibration, light, and radiation must take measures to minimize them in accordance with environmental standards.

4. It is prohibited to manufacture, import, transport, sell, and use firecrackers. The Prime Minister shall decide the manufacture, import, transport, sale, and use of firework.

Actions Against Establishments Causing Serious Environmental Pollution

1. An establishment causing serious environmental pollution means any establishment that discharges wastewater, exhaust gases, dust, solid wastes, noise, vibration, and other pollutants beyond the permissible limits to a serious extent.

2. Establishments causing serious environmental pollution shall incur penalties for administrative violations, be compelled to take measures for pollution removal, and be put on the list of establishments causing serious environmental pollution.

General Regulations On Environmental Pollution Reduction And Classification Of Polluted Areas

1. Pollution reduction means minimization of impacts of pollution on the environment and humans, improvement of environmental quality in the polluted area.

2. Polluted areas shall be classified as pollution, serious pollution, and particularly serious pollution

Pollution Reduction And Environmental Remediation

1. Determination of a polluted area includes:

a) Determine the boundary of the polluted area;

b) Determination of the pollution level and risk assessment;

c) Determination or causes and accountability or relevant parties;

d) Solutions for pollution removal and environmental remediation;

dd) Determination of damage as the basis for claiming compensation.

2. Environment improvement and remediation plan of mining projects must be approved before such projects are put into operation; environmental remediation deposit shall be paid. An environment improvement and remediation plan consists of:

a) Ability, scale, and level of environmental pollution;

b) Risk assessment;

c) Feasible solution for environmental remediation;

d) Plan and budget for environmental remediation.

Pollution Reduction And Environmental Remediation

Organizations and individuals are obliged to:

a) Find a feasible solution for environmental remediation when executing projects likely to cause environmental pollution;

b) Take measures for pollution reduction and environmental improvement when causing environmental pollution;

c) If environmental pollution is caused by multiple entities without responsibility attributed, the environment authority shall cooperate with relevant entities to attribute responsibility for pollution reduction and environmental remediation of each entity.

Preventing Environmental Emergencies

Owners of manufacturing establishments, business establishments or vehicles at risk of causing environmental emergencies shall take the following measures:

a) Make plans for preventing and responding to environmental emergencies;

b) Install equipment and devices serving response to environmental emergencies;

c) Provide training for intramural environmental emergency response teams;

d) Carry out regular inspections and implement safety measures as prescribed by law;

d) Take measures to eliminate the causes of environmental emergencies when finding any sign of environmental emergencies.

Environmental Emergency Response

1. Responsibility for environmental emergency response

a) Any entity that causes an environmental emergency shall take emergency measures to ensure safety of people and property; rescue people and property, then notify the local government or a local agency specialized in environmental protection;

b) The head of the establishment and administrative division where the environmental emergency occurs shall promptly mobilize forces, equipment and vehicles to emergency response;

c) If an environmental emergency occurs to many establishments or administrative divisions, the heads of such establishments and administrative divisions shall cooperate with each other in emergency response;

d) If the situation is beyond the capability of them, the heads shall request the superior agency to mobilize forces from other establishments or administrative divisions to environmental emergency response; the requested establishments or administrative divisions shall implement the emergency response measures within their competence.

2. Response to particularly serious environmental emergencies shall be carried out in accordance with regulations of law on state of emergencies.

3. Manpower, supplies, and vehicles for environmental emergency response shall be reimbursed in accordance with law.

4. Law on environmental protection and relevant regulations of law shall apply to responsibility for paying compensation for environmental emergencies.

Developing Environmental Emergency Response Forces

1. Manufacturing and business establishments shall improve their ability to prevent and respond to environmental emergencies.

2. The State shall develop environmental emergency response forces and environmental emergency warning system.

3. Investment in emergency response services is encouraged.

Determination Of Damage Caused By Environmental Emergencies

The investigation into damage caused by an environmental emergency shall deal with:

a) Determine the boundary of the area polluted because of the environmental emergency;

b) Pollution levels;

c) Causes and accountability or relevant parties;

d) Measures for pollution reduction and environmental remediation;

dd) Damage to the environment as the basis for claiming compensation.

Responsibility For Environmental Remediation

1. Any entity that causes an environmental emergency is obliged to:

a) Comply with the requests of environment authorities during the investigations to determine the pollution scale, levels, and remedial measures.

b) Immediately take measures to prevent the pollution sources, stop the pollution from spreading and affecting local people's health;

c) Take measures for pollution reduction environmental remediation at the request of environment authorities.

d) Pay damages in accordance with Law on environmental protection and relevant regulations;

dd) Submit reports on environmental emergency response and environmental remediation to environment authorities.

2. If the environmental emergency is caused by multiple entities and they fail to reach an agreement on responsibility, the environment authority shall cooperate with relevant entities to attribute responsibility for pollution reduction and environmental remediation of each entity.

3. If the environmental emergency is caused by a natural disaster or an unknown cause, competent authorities shall mobilize forces to carry out pollution reduction and environmental remediation.

Environmental Technical Regulation System

1. Technical regulations on surrounding environment quality include:

a) Environmental technical regulations on soil

b) Environmental technical regulations on surface water and underground water;

c) Environmental technical regulations on sea water;

d) Environmental technical regulations on air;

d) Environmental technical regulations on sound, light, and radiation;

e) Environmental technical regulations on noise, vibration;

2. Technical regulations on waste:

a) Technical regulations on wastewater from industries, services, breeding, aquatic production, domestic, traffic and other activities;

b) Technical regulations on exhaust gas from mobile and fixed sources;

c) Technical regulations on hazardous waste

3. Other technical regulations

Principles Of Constructing Environmental Technical Regulations

1. Meeting goals of environmental protection; preventing, remedying environmental pollution, degradation and problem.

2. Being feasible, suitable for socio-economic development, technological level of the country, and meeting requirements of international economic integration.

3. Being suitable for characteristics of area, regions and production industries

4. Local technical regulations must be stricter than national technical regulations or meet requirements of specifically designed environmental management.

Requirements For Technical Regulations On Surrounding Environment Quality

1. Technical regulations on surrounding environmental quality which regulates the threshold limit value of the environmental factor suitable for use of environmental components include:

a) Minimum value of the environmental factors that ensures life and normal growth of human and living beings;

b) Permissible maximum value of the environmental factors that serves not to cause any negative effect on life and normal growth of human and living beings.

2. Technical regulations on surrounding environmental quality must provide guidance on standard method for measuring, sampling and analysis to determine environmental factors.

Requirements For Technical Regulations On Waste

1. Technical regulations on waste must specifically regulate maximum amount of pollutants contained in the waste ensuring that they cannot cause environmental pollution.

2. Amount of pollutants contained in the waste is determined by relying on the nature of toxicity, quantity of generated waste and loading capacity of the waste receiving environment.

3. Technical regulations on waste must provide guidance on standard method for sampling, measurement and analysis to determine amount of pollutants.

Environmental Standards

1. Environmental standards include standards on surrounding environmental quality, waste and other standards.

2. Whole or part of the environmental technical regulations becomes compulsorily applicable when it is cited from legal documents and environmental technical regulations.

3. Applicable entity standards within management of the standard promulgating agency.

Environmental Monitoring

1. Environmental protection agencies and organizations organize the implementation of surrounding environmental monitoring.

2. The Ministry of Natural Resources and Environment promulgates the list and guides the implementation of emission monitoring with respect to production, business and service entities at risk of imposing effects on the environment.

3. Production, business and service entities which are not on the list of entities responsible for emission monitoring must ensure their compliance with environmental technical regulations and relevant regulations.

Environmental Components And Emissions To Be Monitored

1. Water includes surface water, underground water and sea water.

2. Air includes indoor and outdoor air.

3. Noise, vibration, radiation and light.

4. Soil and deposits

5. Nuclear radiation

6. Wastewater, exhaust gas and solid waste.

7. Hazardous chemicals emitted and built up in the environment.

8. Biological diversity.

Environmental Monitoring Program

1. National environmental monitoring program includes environmental monitoring programs at inter-provincial river and lake basins, key economic zones, trans-border, and geographically distinct zones.

2. Provincial environmental monitoring program includes monitoring programs on environmental components in the area.

3. Environmental monitoring program of industrial parks, export processing zones, high-tech zones, industrial complex, trade villages and production, business and service facilities includes monitoring programs on emissions and environmental components in accordance with the law.

Environmental Monitoring System

1. Environmental monitoring system includes:

a) National environmental monitoring;

b) Provincial environmental monitoring;

c) Intramural environmental monitoring.

2. Organizations involved in the environmental monitoring system include:

a) Organizations in charge of on-site sampling and measurements;

b) Sample analyzing laboratories;

c) Monitoring equipment inspecting and standardizing organizations;

d) Data management and handling, monitoring result establishing and reporting organizations.

3. Environmental monitoring system must be synchronized and interconnected to create a consistent and comprehensive network.

Environmental Information

1. Environmental information includes figures, data about environmental components, environmental impacts, policies and law on environment and environmental protection.

2. Environmental database is a collection of information about the environment being constructed, updated and maintained to meet the demands for access and use of information for environmental protection tasks and for the public interests.

Collection And Management Of Environmental Information

1. The Ministry of Natural Resources and Environment actively coordinates with the ministerial, departmental and local levels to collect and manage environmental information, construct national environmental database.

2. Ministries, departments and people's committees of all levels, within their own duties and authorities, collect and manage environmental information, construct ministerial, departmental and local environmental database and integrate them into the national environmental database.

3. Industrial parks, export processing zones, high-tech zones, industrial complex, trade villages and production, business and service bases prepare environmental dossiers; manage information of environmental impacts from activities of production, business and service.

Publishing Of Environmental Information

1. Environmental information to be made known in public includes:

a) Strategic environmental assessment report, environmental impact assessment report and environmental protection plan;

b) Information of emission sources, emissions and treatment of waste;

c) Areas suffering from serious and particularly serious pollution, degradation, areas at risk of environmental incident;

d) Environmental reports;

d) Results of environment inspections.

1. Information stipulated in this Paragraph and classified as state secrets is not permitted to be published.

2. The publishing method must ensure convenience for information recipients

3. Information-publishing agencies are legally responsible for accuracy of the information.

State Management On Environmental Protection

1. Constructing, promulgating by authority and organizing the implementation of legal documents on environmental protection, promulgating environmental standard, technical process system.

2. Constructing, directing the implementation of strategies, policies, programs, projects, planning and plans on environment.

3. Organizing, constructing, managing monitoring system; carrying out regular evaluation of environmental conditions, forecasting environmental happenings.

4. Constructing, appraising and approving environmental protection planning; appraising strategic environmental assessment report; appraising, approving environmental impact assessment report and inspecting, endorsing environmental protection works; organizing and endorsing environmental protection plan;

5. Directing, instructing and organizing the implementation of biological diversity preserving activities; managing waste; controlling pollution; improving and restoring the environment.

6. Awarding, extending, revoking environmental licenses, certificates.

7. Investigating, inspecting the execution of the law on environmental protection; Investigating state management responsibilities on environmental protection;

8. Training human force in charge of scientific and environmental management, educating and propagandizing knowledge and law on environmental protection.

9. Organizing study and application of scientific and technological advances in environmental protection.

10. Directing, instructing, inspecting and evaluating the implementation of state budget on environmental protection.

11. Furthering international cooperation in environmental protection.

State Management Responsibilities Of The Government For Environmental Protection

The government is unanimous in state management on environmental protection throughout the country.

State Management Responsibilities Of The People' Committees Of All Levels On Environmental Protection

The people's committees of provinces take the following responsibilities:

a) Constructing, promulgating by authority legal documents, policies, programs, planning, plans on environmental protection;

b) Organizing the implementation of law, strategies, programs, plans and duties on environmental protection;

c) Constructing, managing environmental monitoring system in the locality in suitability with general planning of national environmental monitoring;

d) Organizing appraisal and establishment of environmental report. Communicating, popularizing and educating policies and law on environmental protection;

đ) Organizing appraisal, approval of environmental protection planning, environmental impact assessment report, endorsing completion of environmental protection works, instructing and organizing the inspection of environmental protection plan by authority;

e) Awarding, extending, revoking licenses, certificates of environmental protection by authorities;

g) Inspecting, investigating, handling law violations of environmental protection; settling claims, accusations, petitions concerning environment in accordance with the law on complaints and denunciations.

h) Being responsible to the Government for any serious environmental pollution in the area.

Responsibilities And Rights Of Socio-Political Organizations, Socio-Occupational Organizations

1. Socio-political organizations, socio-occupational organizations take the following responsibilities:

a) Complying with the law on environmental protection;

b) Taking part in activities of environmental protection.

2. Socio-political organizations, socio-occupational organizations have the following rights:

a) Being granted access to and the right to ask for information of environmental protection in accordance with the law;

b) Consulting about projects in relation to its functions, duties and authorities;

c) Consulting, responding on environmental protection to state management agencies and owners of production, business and service entities concerned in accordance with the law;

d) Engaging in activities of investigation into environmental protection at production, business and service entities in relation to its functions, duties and authorities;

đ) Submitting petition to competent authorities for handling violations of the law on environmental protection.

Rights And Obligations Of Local Communities

1. Representatives of local communities under environmental effects of production, business and service entities have the right to ask the owners of those production, business and service entities to provide information of environmental protection through direct dialogs or in writing; organize practical enquiry into environmental protection tasks by production, business and service entities; collect, supply information to competent agencies and take responsibility for the information supplied.

2. Representatives of residential community in the area under environmental effects of production, business and service entities have the right to ask state management agencies concerned to supply results of investigation, inspection and handling of the entities.

3. Representatives of residential community have the right to take part in the evaluation of environmental protection tasks by production, business and service entities; implementing all the measures to protect rights and interests of residential community in accordance with the law.

4. Owners of production, business and service entities must fulfill the requirements of residential community.

Expenditure Of State Budget On Environmental Protection

1. Expenditure on environmental protection includes:

a) Constructing strategies, planning, plans, technical processes, technical instructions, technical economic norms, technical regulations on environment, programs and projects on environmental protection;

b) Appraising environmental protection planning, strategic environmental assessment report;

c) Carrying out environmental monitoring; constructing environmental information and reporting system;

d) Providing supports to tasks of investigation and inspection; controlling and treating environmental pollution, preventing, coping and remedying environmental incidents; managing wastes and preserving biological diversity; Training, communicating about environmental protection; popularizing and evaluating the exercising of the law on environmental protection; furthering international cooperation on environmental protection;

đ) Other environmental protection management activities.

2. Expenditures on the development of environmental protection includes those for construction projects, reformation of waste treatment works, constructing and equipping environmental observing and analyzing stations managed by regulatory agencies; investing in equipment, facilities for preventing, coping and remedying environmental pollution, degradation and incident; coping with climate change; preserving biological diversity; reforming polluted water sources, growing and caring green trees in public places, public utility areas.

3. Developing cost estimation and managing use of state budget for environmental protection are done in accordance with the law on state budget.

Cost Of Environmental Protection

1. Organizations, individuals discharging waste into the environment or causing negative effects on the environment shall pay an environment protection fee.

2. Rate of environmental protection fee depends on:

a) Amount of waste discharged into the environment, scale of negative effects on the environment;

b) Levels of toxicity, levels of hazard for the environment;

c) Capacity of waste-receiving environment.

3. The rate of environmental protection is adjusted to requirements of environmental protection and socio-economic conditions of the country in each stage.

4. Collected environmental protection fees shall be used for environmental protection activities.

Environmental Service Development

The state encourages organizations, individuals to establish environmental service business through bidding, public-private partnership (PPP) in the following areas:

a) Collecting, transporting, recycling and treating waste;

b) Observing, analyzing environmental, assessing environmental treatment;

c) Developing, transferring environmental friendly production technology, environmental technology;

d) Providing environmental consultancy, training, and information;

đ) Carrying out environmental appraisal towards goods, machinery, equipment, and technology;

e) Appraising environmental damage and health;

g) Other environmental protection services

Incentives And Support For Environmental Protection Tasks

1. The state shall provide favors, supports to environmental protection tasks below

a) Constructing domestic wastewater treatment systems;

b) Constructing plants for recycling, treating conventional solid waste, hazardous waste, and waste landfill sites;

c) Constructing environmental monitoring stations;

d) Constructing environmental industrial bases, environmental protection works for the benefits of public interests;

đ) Manufacturing and trading eco-friendly products;

e) Transforming operation of industrial parks, industrial complex, and entities causing serious pollution to the environment.

Development And Application Of Science And Technology To Environmental Protection

1. Organizations, individuals involved in the study, transfer, development and application of science and technology to environmental protection shall enjoy favors and supports.

2. Favored activities of study, transfer, development and application of technology to environmental protection include:

a) Studying, transferring, developing and applying technology of waste recycling;

b) Studying, transferring, developing and applying environmental friendly technology and exploiting technology, making effective use of natural resources, saving energy, preserving nature and biological diversity;

c) Studying, transferring, developing and applying waste treatment technology, preventing, minimizing pollution; reforming, restoring and improving environmental quality;

d) Studying, transferring, developing and applying pollution control technology, environmental change forecasting and warning technology; observing and assessing environmental quality;

đ) Studying and constructing facilities to cope with climate change;

e) Studying and applying measures to improve environmental health, minimize environmental impact on people.

Environmental Industry Development

The state shall invest and provide favors and supports to individuals, organizations being involved in the development of environmental industry; in the construction and upgrading of technical infrastructure for waste treatment and recycling; in the establishment and development of centralized waste treatment and recycling sites; in the production and supply of equipment, products in service of environmental protection.

Provision Of Environmental Education And Provision Of Training For Environmental Protection Forces

1. Curriculum of general education levels shall convey environmental content.

2. The state put priority on training human resource for environmental protection; encouraging every organization, individual to participate in the education of environment and training human resource for environmental protection.

Environmental Protection During International Economic Integration

1. The state shall encourage bodies, organizations, and individuals to actively meet the requirements of environment in order to enhance competitiveness of goods and services on regional and international markets.

2. Agencies, organizations, and individuals participating in international economic integration shall be responsible for preventing and minimizing negative impact on domestic environment.

Actions Against Violations

1. Any organization and individual who violates the law on environmental protection causing pollution and degradation to the environment, causing losses to other organizations and individuals shall be responsible for remedying the consequences, restoring the environment, compensating for the damages in accordance with the regulation of Law on environmental protection and relevant laws.

2. Heads of agencies, organizations, officials and public servants who misuse their titles and powers to cause troubles and harassment to organizations, individuals, be involved in cover-ups on violators of environmental protection or show lack of responsibility for environmental pollution and problem, depending on the nature and seriousness of violations, shall incur penalties according to applicable regulations of the law.

Environmental Disputes

1. Environmental disputes include:

a) Disputes concerning rights and responsibilities for environmental protection in exploitation and use of environmental components;

b) Disputes concerning determination of causes to environmental pollution, degradation and problem;

c) Disputes concerning responsibilities for handling and remedying consequences, compensating for losses caused by environmental pollution, degradation and problem.

2. Parties in dispute over environment

a) Organizations, individuals using environmental components in dispute:

b) Organizations, individuals who exploit and use environmental components and organizations, individuals who are responsible for reforming and restoring the polluted and degraded environmental area, and compensating for environmental damages.

3. Settlement of environmental disputes shall be done in accordance with the law on non-contractual civil dispute settlement and the regulation of relevant law.

Complaints, Accusations And Lawsuits

1. Organizations, individuals are entitled to file a complaint and lawsuit against any breach of environmental protection in accordance with the law.

2. Individuals are entitled to report any breach of environmental protection to the authorities according to the law on claims and denunciations.

3. Time limit for filing a lawsuit over environment shall begin when the aggrieved individual's detection of the damage caused by the breach of environmental protection regulations by other organizations, individuals.

Damages Caused By Environmental Pollution And Degradation

Damages caused by environmental pollution and degradation include:

1. Deterioration in environmental function and productivity

2. Loss of human life and health, properties and legal interests of the organizations, individuals due to the deterioration.

Principles Of Handling Responsibilities Of Organizations, Individuals Causing Environmental Pollution

1. Environmental pollution and its consequences shall be studied, investigated and concluded opportunely by regulatory authorities.

2. Any act causing environmental pollution, degradation committed by organizations, individuals shall be handled opportunely according to the law.

3. Principles of handling responsibilities shall be defined as follows:

a) Head of the organization shall take responsibility for any breach of environmental protection relating to activity of his/her organization.

b) Organizations, individuals causing environmental pollution, degradation shall be responsible for remedying the consequences and compensating for the damages caused.

c) In case any individual that causes environmental pollution, degradation during the execution of the tasks assigned by his/her organization, the organization shall be responsible for compensating for damages caused according to the law.

Determination Of Damages Caused By Environmental Pollution, Degradation

1. Degrees of deterioration in environmental function and productivity are as below:

a) Mild

b) Serious

c) Alarming level

2. Determination of scope, area of the environment under deterioration in function and productivity includes:

a) Scope and area of zone and core zone under critical and particularly critical deterioration;

b) Scope, area of buffer zone under direct deterioration;

c) Scope, area of other areas under the impact of core zone and buffer zone.

3. Determination of environmental components under deterioration includes:

a) Determination of number of environmental components under deterioration, categories of ecosystem similar to damaged one;

b) Degree of damage to each environmental component, ecosystem and categories.

4. Calculation of environmental damages is defined as follows:

a) Initial and lasting damages due to deterioration in function and productivity of environmental components;

b) Cost for environmental treatment, reformation and restoration;

c) Cost for minimizing or eliminating damage-causing sources

d) Making enquiries from relevant entities;

5. Calculation of damages due to deterioration in environmental function and productivity is done independently or with coordination of the damage causing party and affected party.

In case either or both of the parties have requests, environmental protection agencies are responsible for instructing the calculation to determine the damages or witnessing determination of damages.

6. Determination of damages to human life and health, properties and legal interests of organizations, individuals caused by environmental pollution and degradation is done in accordance with the law.

Determination Of Damages Caused By Deterioration In Environmental Function And Productivity

1. Appraisal of damages caused by deterioration in environmental function and productivity is done at the request of organizations, individuals affected or the agency involved in settling damage compensation.

2. Foundations for appraising damages include a written proposal for damage compensation, information, data, evidence and others in relation to the compensation and damage causing subject.

3. Deciding on a damage appraising organization shall be jointly agreed by both parties; in case both parties fail to come to an agreement, the decision on the damage appraising organization shall be made by the agency assigned for settling damage compensation.

Liability Insurance For Environmental Damages

1. The State encourages insurance businesses to undertake liability insurance for environmental damages.

2. The State encourages organizations, individuals operating in production, business and service to buy liability insurance for environmental damages.

3. Organizations, individuals operating in production, business and service who are at risk of causing significant damage to the environment must buy liability insurance for environmental damages in accordance with the law of the Government.

Conclusion

Thank you again for downloading this book on *"LAW ON ENVIRONMENTAL PROTECTION: Essential Legal Terms Explained You Need To Know About Law On Environmental Protection!"* and reading all the way to the end. I'm extremely grateful.

If you know of anyone else who may benefit from the informative legal words presented in this book, please help me inform them of this book. I would greatly appreciate it.

Finally, if you enjoyed this book and feel that it has added value to your study or career in any way, please take a couple of minutes to share your thoughts and post a REVIEW on Amazon. Your feedback will help me to continue to write the kind of Kindle books that helps you get results. Furthermore, if you write a simple REVIEW with positive words for this book on Amazon, you can help hundreds or perhaps thousands of other readers who may want to enhance their legal vocabulary have a chance getting what they need. Like you, they worked hard for every penny they spend on books. With the information and recommendation you provide, they would be more likely to take action right away. We really look forward to reading your review.

Thanks again for your support and good luck!

If you enjoy my book, please write a POSITIVE REVIEW on amazon.

-- Dr. Peter Johnson --

Check Out Other Books

Go here to check out other related books that might interest you:

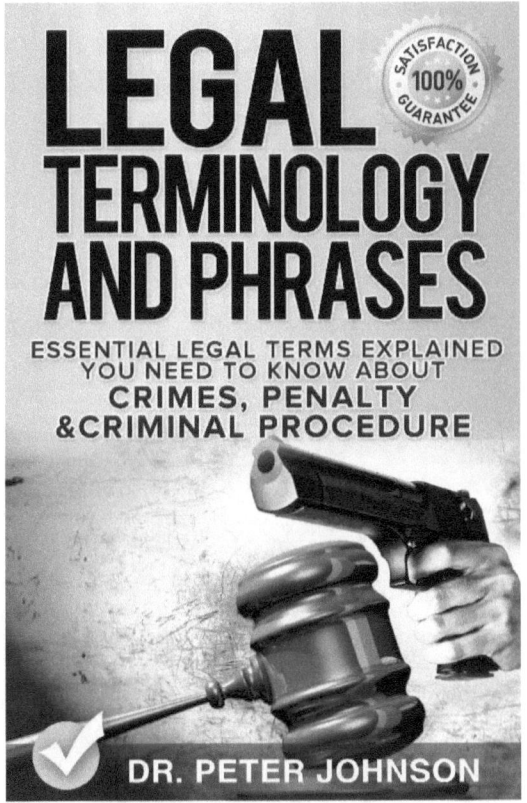

**Legal Terminology And Phrases: Essential Legal Terms Explained
You Need To Know About Crimes, Penalty And Criminal Procedure**

http://www.amazon.com/dp/B01L5EB54Y

LAW ON INTELLECTUAL PROPERTY: Essential Legal Terms
Explained You Need To Know About Trademarks, Copyrights,
Patents, and Trade Secrets!

https://www.amazon.com/dp/B07PFP3MDY

COMPANY LAW: Mastering Essential Legal Terms Explained
About Limited Liability Companies, Joint-Stock Companies,
Partnership, Private Enterprises, And Groups of Companies!

https://www.amazon.com/dp/B07P2PRVMJ

TAX LAW: Essential Legal Terms Explained You Need To Know
About Types of Tax Law!

https://www.amazon.com/dp/B07PH1L3RS

INVESTMENT LAW: Essential Legal Terms Explained You Need To Know About Law On Investment!

https://www.amazon.com/dp/B07P79D925

LABOR LAW: Essential Legal Terms Explained You Need To Know About Law On Labor!

https://www.amazon.com/dp/B07PFD2CML

CIVIL LAW: Mastering Essential Legal Terms Explained About Civil Rights, Guardianship, Civil Transactions, Civil Obligations, Civil Liability, Civil Contracts And Civil Procedure!

https://www.amazon.com/dp/B07P5GS8LD

LAW ON LAWYERS : Essential Legal Terms Explained You Need To Know About Law on Lawyers!

https://www.amazon.com/dp/B07PH9SCBN

Legal Vocabulary In Use: Master 600+ Essential Legal Terms And
Phrases Explained In 10 Minutes A Day

http://www.amazon.com/dp/B01L0FKXPU

Civil Law Vocabulary In Use: Master 350+ Essential Civil Law Terms
And Phrases Explained With Examples In 10 Minutes A Day.

https://www.amazon.com/dp/B0781TQWGV

Criminal Law Vocabulary In Use: Master 400+ Essential Criminal
Law Terms And Phrases Explained With Examples In 10 Minutes A
Day.

https://www.amazon.com/dp/B078KLR51Z

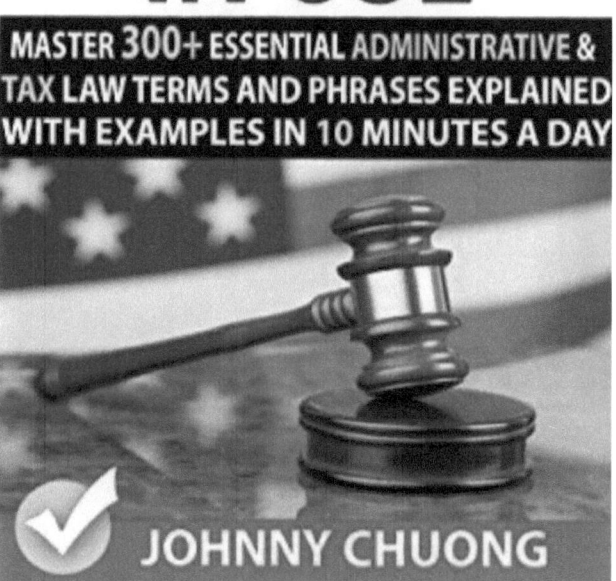

Administrative And Tax Law In Use : Master 300+ Administrative And Tax Law Terms And Phrases Explained With Examples In 10 Minutes A Day.

https://www.amazon.com/dp/B07JMD546J

Productivity Secrets For Students: The Ultimate Guide To Improve Your Mental Concentration, Kill Procrastination, Boost Memory And Maximize Productivity In Study

http://www.amazon.com/dp/B01JS52UT6

Shortcut To Ielts Writing: The Ultimate Guide To Immediately
Increase Your Ielts Writing Scores

http://www.amazon.com/dp/B01JV7EQGG